T5-CVG-978

" To Patrick "

From Grandpa
& Grandma Melvin

MOTHER GOOSE
on the Farm

Selected by DIANE MULDROW
Illustrated by AMY AITKEN

A GOLDEN BOOK · NEW YORK

Western Publishing Company, Inc., Racine, Wisconsin 53404

Copyright © 1989 Western Publishing Company, Inc. Illustrations copyright © 1989 Amy Aitken.
All rights reserved. Printed in the U.S.A. No part of this book may be reproduced or copied
in any form without written permission from the publisher. GOLDEN®, GOLDEN & DESIGN®,
A GOLDEN TELL-A-TALE® BOOK, and A GOLDEN BOOK® are trademarks of Western Publishing
Company, Inc. Library of Congress Catalog Card Number: 88-51880   ISBN: 0-307-07060-3
C D E F G H I J K L M

The Cock's on the Housetop

The cock's on the housetop blowing his horn;
The bull's in the barn a-threshing of corn.
The maids in the meadows are making of hay;
The ducks in the river are swimming away.

Cocks Crow

Cocks crow in the morn
To tell us to rise,
And he who lies late
Will never be wise.

For early to bed
And early to rise
Is the way to be healthy
And wealthy and wise.

Elsie Marley

Elsie Marley is grown so fine,
She won't get up to feed the swine,
But lies in bed till eight or nine,
And surely she does take her time.

I Bought a Dozen New-Laid Eggs

I bought a dozen new-laid eggs
Of good old farmer Dickens.
I hobbled home upon two legs
And found them full of chickens.

Little Boy Blue

Little Boy Blue, come blow your horn!
The sheep's in the meadow, the cow's in the corn.
Where's the boy that looks after the sheep?
He's under the haystack, fast asleep.
Will you wake him? No, not I,
For if I do, he's sure to cry.

Cow, Cow

Cow, cow, come blow your horn,
And you shall have a peck of corn.

Bow-wow, Says the Dog

"Bow-wow," says the dog;
"Mew, mew," says the cat;
"Grunt, grunt," goes the hog;
And "Squeak," goes the rat.

"To-who," says the owl;
"Caw, caw," says the crow;
"Quack, quack," says the duck;
And "Moo," says the cow.

Little Bo-Peep

Little Bo-Peep has lost her sheep
And can't tell where to find them.
Leave them alone, and they'll come home
And bring their tails behind them.

If I Had a Mule, Sir

If I had a mule, sir, and he wouldn't start,
Do you think I'd harness him up to a cart?
No, no, I'd give him oats and hay
And let him stay there all the day.

March Winds

March winds and April showers
Bring forth May flowers.

Summer Breeze

Summer breeze, so softly blowing,
In my garden pinks are growing.
If you go and send the showers,
You may come and smell my flowers.

Ply the Spade

Ply the spade
And ply the hoe,
Plant the seed
And it will grow.

Harvest Home

Harvest home, harvest home,
Ne'er a load's been overthrown.

Cock-a-Doodle-Do!

Cock-a-doodle-do!
My dame has lost her shoe.
My master's lost his fiddlestick
And knows not what to do.

Dickory, Dickory, Dare

Dickory, dickory, dare,
The pig flew up in the air.
The man in brown soon brought him down,
Dickory, dickory, dare.

The Miller He Grinds

The miller is grinding his corn, his corn,
    The miller is grinding his corn.
The little boy blue comes winding his horn,
    With a hop and a step and a jump.

The damsels are churning for curds and whey,
    The damsels are churning for whey.
The lads in the field are making the hay,
    With a hop and a step and a jump.

Baa, Baa, Black Sheep

Baa, baa, black sheep, have you any wool?
Yes, sir, yes, sir, three bags full:
One for my master, one for my dame,
And one for the little boy that lives in our lane.

Pitty Patty Polt

Pitty Patty Polt,
Shoe the wild colt.
Here a nail
And there a nail,
Pitty Patty Polt.

A Cat Came Fiddling

A cat came fiddling out of a barn
With a pair of bagpipes under her arm.
She could sing nothing but fiddle-de-dee,
The mouse has married the bumblebee.
Pipe, cat, dance, mouse—
We'll have a wedding at our good house.

Oh, Dear!

Oh, dear! What can the matter be?
  Two old women got up in an apple tree.
One came down, and the other stayed till Saturday.

Sleep, Baby, Sleep

Sleep, baby, sleep,
Our cottage vale is deep.
The little lamb is on the green
With woolly fleece so soft and clean—
Sleep, baby, sleep.

The Cat and the Fiddle

Hey, diddle, diddle!
The cat and the fiddle,
The cow jumped over the moon.
The little dog laughed to see such sport,
And the dish ran away with the spoon.

Bossy-cow, Bossy-cow

Bossy-cow, bossy-cow, where do you lie?
In the green meadow, under the sky.

Billy-horse, billy-horse, where do you lie?
Out in the stable, with nobody nigh.

Birdies bright, birdies sweet, where do you lie?
Up in the treetops—oh, ever so high!

Baby dear, baby love, where do *you* lie?
In my warm crib, with mama nearby.